THE FIRST BOOK OF

An introduction

PAINTINGS

to the appreciation of pictures

by LAMONT MOORE

FRANKLIN WATTS, Inc.

575 Lexington Avenue · New York 22

THE author and publisher are indebted to Mr. Laurence Sickman of the William Rockhill Nelson Gallery of Art and the Atkins Museum of Fine Arts, Kansas City, Missouri, for permission to use the poem on page 8, from *Art and Architecture of China,* by Laurence Sickman and Alexander Soper, Penguin Books, 1956.

*

TITLE PAGE ILLUSTRATION: *The Artist in his Studio,* by JAN VERMEER. Courtesy of the Kunsthistorisches Museum, Vienna, Austria.

*

DESIGNED BY CHARLES FARRELL

CONTENTS ❧

❧ CONTENTS

ARTISTS REPRESENTED IN THIS BOOK ❧

ANGELICO, FRA (1387–1455)
BOTTICELLI, SANDRO (1444?–1510)
BRUEGHEL, PIETER THE ELDER (1520?–1569)
CÉZANNE, PAUL (1839–1906)
CONSTABLE, JOHN (1776–1837)
EXEKIAS (Sixth century B.C.)
EYCK, JAN VAN (1370?–1440?)
GIORGIONE (Giorgio Barbarelli) (1480?–1511)
GOGH, VINCENT VAN (1853–1890)
GRECO, EL (Domenikos Theotokopoulos) (1548?–1614?)
HARUNOBU, SUZUKI (c. 1718–1770)
HOBBEMA, MEINDERT (1638–1709)
HOMER, WINSLOW (1836–1910)
LEONARDO DA VINCI (1452–1519)
LORRAIN, CLAUDE (1600–1682)
MONDRIAN, PIET CORNELIS (1872–1944)
MONET, CLAUDE (1840–1926)
PICASSO, PABLO (1881–   )
RAPHAEL (Raffaello Santi) (1483–1520)
REMBRANDT VAN RIJN (1606–1669)
RENOIR, AUGUSTE (1841–1919)
ROUSSEAU, HENRI-JULIEN (1844–1910)
RYDER, ALBERT PINKHAM (1847–1917)
SASSETTA (Stefano di Giovanni) (1392–1450)
SEURAT, GEORGES (1859–1891)
SHÊN CHOU (1427–1509)
VAN DYCK, SIR ANTHONY (1599–1641)
VELÁZQUEZ, DIEGO RODRÍGUEZ DE SILVA Y (1599–1660)
VERMEER, JAN (1632–1675)
WATTEAU, JEAN ANTOINE (1684–1721)
WHISTLER, JAMES ABBOTT McNEILL (1834–1903)

T HE WORD "art" comes from a Latin word that the ancient Romans used when they wanted to say "skill." A work of art is, therefore, a work of skill. It may be a building constructed of stone or concrete, a piece of sculpture made of stone or metal or carved from wood, or a picture painted with brushes and colors on canvas cloth or a plaster wall. Works of art are created by artists, people born with a talent for making things. Usually they spend many years developing their talents as they learn to use the materials and tools of their profession. It might seem then that any talented person, skillful with his hands and well-trained, could be an artist. This is not the case. An artist must be born with a *gift of seeing*.

We all see the world around us. The sky is filled with stars, the earth with rocks and trees, birds and animals, people, cities—thousands of things. We learn to recognize these things and we go through life looking at them with our eyes, but we do not necessarily think much about them or comprehend them.

The artist sees with his eyes and perceives with his mind much more clearly than we do. His gift of seeing and his trained skill combine in his art to show us the world. He not only shows us the world; he also tells us how he feels about it.

When an artist paints a sunset, for example, he lets us know whether he was uplifted by the sight of the glowing colors or whether he felt sad that the day was ending. A work of art must reveal how the artist thought and felt when he created it.

An artist may select anything as a subject—a tree, a river, a room, a person—just as an author selects a subject for a story. The artist gives us the appearance of what he has chosen, but in order to express his feeling he must emphasize something: the curve of a branch, the expression in a person's eyes, the color of a flower. As soon as he stresses one part of his subject, he is changing the appearance, very slightly or possibly a great deal. Art is not an exact copy of what the artist sees. Art begins when the artist departs from strict imitation in order to tell us how he feels and what he thinks about his subject.

This book is an introduction to the art of painting. If you will glance through the pages, you will see that artists have seen things in many different ways. But they have all used the same elements and the same principles to create their pictures. The elements, the basic things used in making a painting, are *line, shape, space, light,* and *color.* The principles, the basic rules, which the artist follows in using the five elements have to do with *pattern, balance, rhythm, contrast* and *unity.* The elements and principles have a bearing on all the arts, not just on painting alone.

We tell each other what we feel by using words; we speak a language. A painting is silent. The artist uses the language of art to tell us what he wants to say. The ''words'' of the language are the elements and principles. If we become acquainted with them, we can better understand the art of painting. Understanding brings appreciation, and appreciation brings pleasure.

MAN BEGAN making paintings thousands of years ago when he lived in caves. One of the animals roaming the earth at that time was the woolly rhinoceros. Here he is as he was painted on the wall of a cave in southern France. The hunter-artist worked by the light of a small stone lamp, with paints made from crumbled colored rocks. He outlined clearly the animal he had observed so carefully while hunting.

Line is the beginning of painting. It shows us the edge of shape. It can be continuous or broken, thick or thin, clear and hard or smudged and soft, dark and heavy or very faint and delicate.

Look at the tail of the animal, and move your eyes along its back. Strong continuous line becomes fuzzy and then stops. Four short strokes mark a topknot of fur. The line starts again, spreads out into the horns with their knifelike edges, becomes thin and crisp at the mouth, and then vague once more along the jaws. Short lines indicate the long hair of the animal's belly. By different kinds of line the cave man showed us what impressed him most about a woolly rhinoceros: his strong back, his sharp horns, his long fur.

You can see that the painting was finished with a few short strokes running forward and downward from the line of the back to show us that the animal had a rounded shape. Line directs our eyes to whatever part of the picture the artist wants us to be sure to notice. The lines in this painting point to the business end of the rhinoceros: his head and horns.

Line in painting often suggests movement, also. If you would like to try an interesting experiment, take a sheet of thin paper and lay it over the picture. Follow the outline of the rhinoceros with a soft pencil; don't bear down hard. Change the direction of the short lines along the back. Make them go the opposite way. Do the same for the fur along the animal's belly. You will see that the effect of movement will be quite different.

Woolly Rhinoceros
Font-de-Gaume Cave, France

VINCENT VAN GOGH, a Dutch artist, lived quite recently. He painted with forceful line, as strong and clear as the cave artist's. He placed his lines next to each other, however, so that they form the shapes in his pictures as well as the edges. You can see in *The Starry Night* that the lines are nearly all of the same thickness. They are painted row upon row on the hills, which seem to march from left to right.

The lines curve this way and that except on the roofs of the houses and church, whose spire points to heaven. The lines waver back and forth in the tall, dark cypress trees that also point skyward. The artist was fond of these trees and painted them many times as if they were stirred by the wind and actually growing, thrusting themselves up from the earth. He wrote in one of his letters, "Cypresses interest me continuously. I should like to paint them like my sunflowers. I am indeed surprised that nobody has seen them as I do."

Van Gogh was a deeply religious man who loved the world and broad sky by day or night. He painted the moon and stars like blinding lights whirling through space, because in his painting he wanted us to marvel at the beauty of the night as he marveled when he painted it. He ringed the moon and every star with lines of radiance, and linked them with swirls suggesting the great path of the Milky Way. We know we cannot see the stars just as they appear in this picture. The artist departed from appearances to tell us of his pleasure, joy, and excitement with line that expressed these feelings.

The Starry Night   VINCENT VAN GOGH
The Museum of Modern Art, New York
ACQUIRED THROUGH THE LILLIE P. BLISS BEQUEST

SHÊN CHOU was a Chinese painter and poet. He lived in the country and was content with his simple life. He painted, wrote, read books, and studied nature. He said that news of worldly affairs did not enter his gate. If it intruded, the breeze in the pines wafted it away.

We can imagine that one day he walked to the top of a mountain. He looked out from the height, and a poem came to his mind. He returned to his home and wrote the poem, using paper, ink, and a brush rather than a pen. After finishing the poem, he decided to paint a picture of his experience on the mountain. He might have used the same brush and ink as for the poem. Once he touched the paper with the brush, he could not change what he had made. But he had practiced to become a skillful painter. He placed the lines surely and quickly.

On the right he painted dark pines, with twisting lines for trunks and branches and little dabs of ink for clusters of needles. His lines show us the edges of shapes and the shapes themselves. Like van Gogh, he expressed his feeling for the trees. They point down into the valley and cling to the hard rocks. Washing much water and just a little ink on the paper, he surrounded the high cliff on which he stood with clouds of mist. Shên Chou finished his picture by writing his poem in the upper left portion of the sky.

White clouds encircle the mountain waist like a sash,
Stone steps mount high into the void where the narrow path leads far.
Alone, leaning on my rustic staff, I gaze idly into the distance.
My longing for the notes of a flute is answered in the murmurings of the gorge.

Poet on a Mountain　　　　　　　　　　　　SHÊN CHOU

Nelson Gallery–Atkins Museum of Fine Arts (NELSON FUND)
Kansas City, Missouri

Sandro Botticelli, an Italian painter, has been compared with oriental artists because he drew and painted with such beautiful line. He outlined shapes with curving line and focused attention on important parts of his pictures. If you make an imaginary X to the four corners of this painting, you will see that the poses taken by the figures, the placing of their heads and hands, and the curving lines of their robes direct your eyes to the Mother and Child. The group of spirited horses restrained by the men does not distract from the focal point in the center.

There are over forty people in the picture. They are grouped so harmoniously that the painting seems spacious and we enjoy the distant view of the Italian countryside. The sections of ruined buildings that frame the central scene were not invented by the artist. When he was living, there were many ancient Roman ruins in Italy. Some remain to the present day.

The faces are those of the townspeople of Florence, where the artist worked, and of the famous Medici family who ruled the city at that time. This picture included both landscape and portraits in addition to the religious theme.

Botticelli also made pen and ink drawings to illustrate Italian books. The sketches are filled with the same flowing and graceful lines that we see in his paintings.

Line is the edge of shape and the divider between one shape and another. Line directs our eyes through a picture and expresses life and movement.

The Adoration of the Magi
National Gallery of Art, Washington, D. C.
MELLON COLLECTION

SANDRO BOTTICELLI

Shape made simply by an enclosing line has height and width. Essentially it is flat, and well suited for the decoration of a wall or the smooth surface of a vase, as we see on the opposite page. EXEKIAS, a painter of ancient Greece, recorded a festive wedding. Each figure is a flat shape edged with a finely drawn line. We imagine that one figure is behind another. The artist helped our imagination. For example, he painted one of the horses white and in that way showed us that the chariot was drawn by two pairs of horses. If all four had been painted black, we might have had some difficulty in telling them apart. The same thing is true of the faces of the men and women.

The bride is driving. The groom stands next to her. A goddess faces them, and behind the horses stands a god, presumably Apollo with his lyre. We enjoy not only the beautiful lines that created the shapes but also the fine details of the designs on the dresses and the different hair styles. But of greatest importance are the shapes themselves. They fill precisely and elegantly the wide band encircling the vase.

Ancient artists were accustomed to show figures in profile: that is, they showed the side view of a person rather than the front view. You can make a profile drawing in this way. Put a piece of paper on the wall and ask a friend to sit sideways in front of it; then shine a light on his head and draw around the shadow cast on the paper.

Greek Vase

Courtesy of the Metropolitan Museum of Art, New York

ROGERS FUND, 1917

EXEKIAS

FRA ANGELICO, an Italian monk, painted a fresco directly on the wall of the monastery. He had been well taught and was skillful in the placing of the figures, which he outlined simply and gracefully.

We feel that the angel has come from heaven through the lovely landscape that Fra Angelico placed on the left-hand side of the picture. Through the archway we have a glimpse of trees, a fence, and flowers. The angel has splendid wings and is kneeling, leaning toward Mary who is seated on the other side of the picture. Each arch acts as a framing shape to set off the figure within. The two arches share the same central column, so that both halves of the painting fit together.

The artist emphasized the vaulted ceiling of the porch with curved shadows the same shape as the angel's wings. The shadows lead our eyes over to Mary. In contrast to the angel, she sits almost in the center of her arch. The curves of the vaulting lead our eyes to her face. Behind her is a little straight-sided door, and an empty room with a tiny window, a retreat from the world.

The knowledge of the art of painting had grown a great deal since the time of the Greek vase painters. Fra Angelico painted according to methods that had been worked out to give space and depth. He used light and shade, but even so his figures are simple and quite flat. They seem only half-rounded. The line on the floor of the porch suggests depth and distance, a suggestion called *perspective*.

In a way, Fra Angelico's paintings are like large versions of the pictures in medieval books. They tell the stories of the Bible in a charming manner.

Annunciation

San Marco Museum, Florence, Italy

FRA ANGELICO

SEVERAL HUNDRED years after Fra Angelico, the French artist AUGUSTE RENOIR also painted a porch scene. We see a group of young men and women who have been boating on the river and have enjoyed their luncheon on the shore. Everybody is happy and relaxed.

Here the artist has skillfully blended together a great variety of shapes: the shapes of the bottles, glasses, and fruits on the table, the poses of the people themselves, and particularly the hats they are wearing, each one of them a different shape. The figures extend across the front of the picture and recede toward the back. They are fully rounded, not half-round like the figures in the *Annunciation*.

So well did Renoir master the elements of painting—*line, shape, space, light,* and *color*—that he could devote his attention to the individuals in the picture. Each one seems to be a portrait sketch of one or another of his friends. He was interested in the expressions on their faces: the wistful look of the girl leaning on the railing, for example.

He included many different episodes in the scene. The lady on the left is talking to her little dog perched in front of her on the table. A girl farther back on the porch is drinking from a glass. The woman with black gloves arranges her hair while the young men stand in admiration. All in all, *Luncheon of the Boating Party* is the description of a lively and informal afternoon, told with great attention to detail and with masterful grouping of many different space-filling shapes.

Luncheon of the Boating Party   Auguste Renoir

Phillips Collection, Washington, D. C.

WE HAVE SEEN how Renoir created a picture of men and women chatting after their luncheon. He was interested in the people, but painted carefully the bottles, glasses, and fruit. If another French artist, PAUL CÉZANNE, had been there that afternoon, it is quite likely that he would have painted only the "still life" on the table. He would have done it after the people had gone, because he needed a great deal of time and concentration to produce a picture such as the one on the opposite page.

Cézanne has been called the "father of modern art" because he decided to start painting as if none had been done before him. He worked on the problems of each element in painting and tried to solve them slowly in a careful way. He was particularly interested in conveying the feeling of solidity and depth that is well illustrated here. He emphasized the shapes of everything: the apples, the glass bottles, the folds of the dark piece of cloth with leaf design, and the folds of the white cloth on top. But he has done much more than tell us just how round or how thick these objects are. He has made us feel their weight. The full shapes are crowded into a group near the center; the stiff, heavy folds of the cloths move and swirl around them. Behind, to the left and right, are a flat wall and floor, with a dark, vertical shape suggesting either a closed or open door.

Cézanne painted landscapes and people with a similar type of clear-cut form, which makes them look impressive and eternal.

Still Life

PAUL CÉZANNE

National Gallery of Art, Washington, D. C.
CHESTER DALE COLLECTION

SHAPES can be small in a picture such as the Chinese painting on page 9, or they can be large, as in the *Luncheon of the Boating Party*. And shapes can occupy different kinds of *space*.

In ancient Roman times an unknown painter decorated the house of a wealthy man with a fresco showing a wedding scene. The painting was later taken from the wall and became part of the collection of Cardinal Aldobrandini; hence its name. In it are groups of figures in little spaces that are almost like small rooms. The Roman artist has shown the three people on the right slightly smaller, to indicate that they were at the back of the room.

Behind the figures the artist has set walls, but they do not go deeply into the picture. He has limited the space and painted the figures rather small, but not too small. In fact, he has balanced the space and figures so that one is not more important than the other.

How did he achieve his effect? He used two ways of suggesting depth. First, he placed the walls at different angles. These angles are lines of perspective that lead our eyes into the picture. Second, he painted the figures light on the right side and dark on the left. The use of light and shade suggests the air or atmosphere that surrounds each figure, and gives it the appearance of molded shape. You will remember that on the Greek vase the artist painted flat figures.

Even so, the general impression of this Roman painting is quite stiff, rather like a piece of sculpture.

Aldobrandini Marriage
Vatican Museum, Rome, Italy

ABOUT FIFTY YEARS before Columbus discovered America a Belgian artist painted this double portrait of an Italian merchant and his young bride. JAN VAN EYCK portrayed them exchanging vows. You can easily see that he and other artists had learned a great deal about representing space.

The event van Eyck painted takes place in the deep space of a boxlike room unlike the shallow alcoves of the Roman wedding scene. Van Eyck used perspective lines to help create the appearance of depth. The lines are not quite accurate because he was slow to master perspective. But he more than made up for his slight fault. He created the sense of space by using light and shade, as well. Light from the window makes shadows and thereby rounded shapes, especially in the folds of cloth. The figure of the young lady even casts a shadow on the coverlet behind her.

This remarkable artist succeeded in showing us the heaviness of fabric, the fineness of fur, the sparkle of light from the mirror, and all other details because he painted as if he were seeing everything through a crystal-clear atmosphere. Van Eyck achieved the highly finished appearance of his portrait by using a new method of painting that he had developed. He used oil to mix colors. With oil paints he could brush over one color with a thin layer of another, permitting the first to show through. In this way he gained deep, rich, glowing effects never before obtained. With oil paints he could also make smooth changes from light to dark in the shapes. They look real to us.

Jan van Eyck signed this painting in an unusual way. You can see, over the mirror, an inscription in Latin: *Jan van Eyck was present*.

The Betrothal of the Arnolfini   JAN VAN EYCK

Reproduced by Courtesy of the Trustees
The National Gallery, London, England

LEONARDO DA VINCI was one of the great artists in history. He was also a scientist, for he carefully examined the way man is constructed as well as all phases of nature: the way plants and trees grow, the movement of clouds, winds, and waves. He studied light, and noted that distant objects seem to have soft, blurred outlines while nearby shapes look sharp and clear. But even these nearby shapes may be softened if the light falls in a certain way or if they are in shadow. Leonardo studied nature so carefully that when he finished painting *Mona Lisa* she seemed to be living and breathing in the emptiness of space, with distant mountains as a background.

Unlike Jan van Eyck, who was intent on painting every small detail, Leonardo has blended sharp lines with veiled shapes that have soft, blurred shadows. By this method of "smokiness," as it is sometimes called, he suggested not only the outward appearance of the lady, but also her inward character. Note especially that the shadows are soft at the corners of her eyes and mouth, and help to create her famous and mysterious smile.

Leonardo and his fellow artists knew how to present shapes so that they appeared to be round and to have space behind them. The figure occupies most of the height and width of this painting. But as we look beyond, on either side of her head, our eyes do not stop until we see the craggy mountains, their tops partly hidden in mist. Space in this picture extends to a tremendous depth.

Mona Lisa   LEONARDO DA VINCI
Louvre, Paris, France

LANDSCAPE ARTISTS deal primarily with space, as this peaceful river scene by the Frenchman CLAUDE LORRAIN shows. Lorrain was the first painter to devote most of his attention to trees, sky, hills, fields, and water. He spent a great deal of time in the countryside near Rome, Italy, and he often sketched there in the soft evening light that gave him the greatest pleasure.

This picture shows a herdsman stopping on the riverbank to remove his shoes before wading across the shallow water. He will follow the cattle as they return homeward at nightfall. The shore line curves away where the river widens. Two fishermen pull in their net loaded with the day's catch. The line of the opposite bank is straight. It leads into the center of the painting where a bridge directs our eyes across to the hill on the right. We look beyond to the distant hills.

The space in the painting opens out to that part of the sky that is lightest and brightest. The artist placed the three large trees with care so that each shows a different silhouette against the sky. Two are seen with their edges blurred by the bright light from the setting sun. Claude Lorrain emphasized the element of space in painting, but he also used the element of *light*.

Light, as an element in painting, reveals shape. We see clearly that an object is bright on the lighted side and dark on the shadowed side. Light also can destroy shape, especially when an object is seen directly in front of a very strong light source.

River Landscape　　　　　　　　　　　　　　　　　　CLAUDE LORRAIN

California Palace of the Legion of Honor, San Francisco, California
MILDRED ANNA WILLIAMS COLLECTION

JAN VERMEER lived in the town of Delft in the Netherlands. He painted this picture of a Dutch girl standing by a window in her home. On the table we see a metal pitcher, a basin, a fancy box, and a richly patterned carpet. The soft light coming through the leaded panes slides down the girl's arm, reflects from her right shoulder, and passes through the thin, starched kerchief over her head. The room seems filled with fresh air and sunshine because the artist knew just how to bring out the objects evenly and clearly. He selected those that had different kinds of surfaces to reflect the light, and he observed their appearance carefully.

Vermeer was a true Dutch artist and painted subjects of everyday life. Even though he gave everything in his pictures the appearance of reality, he softened all the edges ever so slightly as he painted. The wealthy merchants who bought his paintings liked the exact manner in which they were done. He displayed clearly the bright metalwork, and the fabrics and handsome rugs that the merchants had obtained from Eastern countries.

It may be that artists living in the Netherlands are more aware of light because of the vast expanse of sky. As it changes constantly over their heads, the sunny or cloudy effects change the appearance of the flat landscape below. Scientists today tell us that light has shape and substance. Vermeer sensed this fact three hundred years ago. He observed every object in light in a scientific manner. Notice the reflection of the carpet on the under side of the metal basin. This remarkable artist was able to paint a reflection even in shadow.

Young Woman with a Water Jug JAN VERMEER
Courtesy of the Metropolitan Museum of Art, New York
GIFT OF HENRY G. MARQUAND, 1889

CLAUDE LORRAIN filled his landscape with calm, clear evening light. REMBRANDT VAN RIJN, famous painter of the Netherlands, presented nightfall in a different way. A great windmill stands against the sky. The arms of the mill reflect the last rays of sunset. A man is bringing his boat to shore; a woman finishes washing clothes in the stream; a boy stands by, idly watching. A little girl and her mother make their way home. Perhaps the boatman will take them to the opposite shore where we see a church spire outlined faintly above the trees.

Men, women, and children are very small compared with the great rock, the windmill, and the vast expanse of sky. This painting may be a recollection of Rembrandt's own childhood, for he is supposed to have been born and raised in a miller's house. When he grew up, he went to Amsterdam to paint portraits and make his fortune.

In his picture Claude Lorrain painted the light as if it were coming toward us from the setting sun. Rembrandt chose a later time of day, after the sun had set. The afterglow was still brilliant, but beginning to darken. He lighted his scene from the back and side. Whether he was painting a person or a place, Rembrandt made most of his pictures glow with this light that seems to come from within the subject. It reveals shapes. It balances perfectly the deep, transparent shadows.

In such paintings as *The Mill,* Rembrandt paints light as few other artists have been able to, so that it expresses the mystery of space and the majesty of nature. Rembrandt is also famous for his skill in drawing and etching. He made hundreds of illustrations for religious stories. They show his mastery of line as well as of light and shadow.

The Mill

REMBRANDT VAN RIJN

National Gallery of Art, Washington, D. C.
WIDENER COLLECTION

WINSLOW HOMER was one of the greatest American painters, and was well known for his pictures of the sea. In *Fog Warning* we see how well he could paint the effect of light on the ocean.

A fisherman has been out a long time. He has successfully brought two huge fish into his dory and is rowing toward his ship, outlined on the horizon. The fog is rolling in and will soon hide the ship from sight; the captain has sounded a warning. The fisherman pauses in his rowing to glance apprehensively over his shoulder at the sky. If he does not hurry, he will have trouble finding the schooner as the fog advances.

The light comes toward us from the bright sky above the dark fog clouds. The figure of the man is seen against the light and is in silhouette. When we see figures outdoors against bright light, their dark forms appear larger than normal. We feel that this fisherman is strong and will be able to reach the safety of his ship before the fog closes in, but he will have a close race, for the sea is strong also.

Notice the beautiful contrast of the silvery light on the fish and waves in the lower part of the painting and then again on the sharp tips of the waves against the dark sky. The artist has used a principle of perspective to give depth to a scene under an open sky. He alternated light and dark bands across the picture from bottom to top.

The shining light outlines the gunwales of the fisherman's dory, which make a bright frame for his dark form. Winslow Homer knew that strong contrasts of light and dark make a picture exciting, and he used dramatic light appropriately here to tell us a story of suspense.

Fog Warning   WINSLOW HOMER

Courtesy, Museum of Fine Arts, Boston, Massachusetts

A GROUP of French artists became interested in the investigations of the scientists who had been examining light. The artists decided to experiment also. Their leader, CLAUDE MONET, painted the same scene many times at different hours of the day and in both bright and cloudy weather. This view of Rouen Cathedral is one of twenty-six impressions painted at almost the same spot in front of the building.

This particular impression suggests dazzling sunlight moving over the richly carved stonework. Monet painted with short strokes that left little ridges of paint. He left them rough to give texture to the painting, thereby suggesting the brilliance of light reflected back from the many small surfaces on the front of the enormous church. We can tell how big it is by looking at the three dark little shapes of people in the lower left corner.

The painting appears unusual in that it was painted to be viewed from a certain distance. The artist applied his colors in little patches of different hues without blending them together very much. He knew that we would automatically adjust ourselves to the picture. If we are too close, the painting looks flat and jumbled. Hold this book out at arm's length and you will see that the building appears to have more depth in the doorways.

Monet and his associates were called "Impressionists." They painted their impressions of scenes viewed through atmosphere and light. Light had become the most important element in their painting.

Rouen Cathedral, West Façade, Sunlight   CLAUDE MONET
National Gallery of Art, Washington, D. C.
CHESTER DALE COLLECTION

Color is often important in painting. An artist can employ color in several different ways. He can use it to tell us that the grass is green and the roses are red. Then it is descriptive color. It is an added help to line and shape in describing an object. But color can also be the most important element in a painting; it can stir our feelings; or it can decorate the surface of a picture with a pleasing pattern.

SASSETTA used descriptive color in his *Journey of the Magi*. The travelers wear red, blue, yellow, and pink costumes. The hill on the right is gray; the hill on the left is greenish-brown. All the colors go well together and form a pleasing arrangement. The salmon pink buildings are an unusual feature of this color scheme.

Notice how easy it is to see each figure in the various groups. When horses were placed together, Sassetta painted one black, another brown, and another white so that we can see each one clearly. When he came to paint the sky he showed that, although he was working indoors, he had observed the real sky outdoors and knew that the blue changes from light where it joins the land to dark over our heads. We understand from this that painters even as far back in time as Sassetta were beginning to use color to note their impressions of light and air.

Thin sheets of gold were used as color by early Italian artists. The Magi have gold halos, and the Star is gold. Notice that Sassetta did not place the Star in the sky. It floats in the air close to the ground, moving along with the procession, guiding the Wise Men to Bethlehem.

The Journey of the Magi
Courtesy of the Metropolitan Museum of Art, New York
BEQUEST OF MAITLAND F. GRIGGS, 1943

SASSETTA

∾ C O L O R

GIORGIONE was one of several artists in Venice who were famous for their use of color. Because he died when he was only about thirty-five years old, there are very few of his paintings in existence. All of them show that he was a great colorist.

Giorgione placed the figures in *The Adoration of the Shepherds* in the landscape he knew, that part of the Italian coastline near Venice, in the foothills of the mountains where the Venetians had built their summer castles. He used people of the countryside as his models.

You will see that the entire picture has a golden glow. The atmosphere seems to be filled with the color of sunlight. A rich, warm tone comes from sky, trees, and rocks, as well as from the deep, jewel-like colors of the robes. Although the colors are strong they are not harsh, because the artist softened them with effects of light and shade. He used a silvery white to separate colors. It helped to keep them pure and intense. Giorgione knew that certain colors improve each other when they are placed close together. Red improves green. Blue improves orange. He balanced the blue-orange combination on the right by using the same colors in paler tones for the sky on the left.

Compare the red of Mary's robe with the red of the torn sleeve on the shepherd. They are quite different. An artist who is particularly interested in the study of colors varies those he uses. The use of colors in this kind of painting might be compared to the use of notes in music. The chords of color in Giorgione's paintings are deep and strong.

The Adoration of the Shepherds   GIORGIONE

National Gallery of Art, Washington, D. C.

SAMUEL H. KRESS COLLECTION

DOMENIKOS THEOTOKOPOULOS was born near Greece, but lived most of his life in Spain. Since his name was difficult for the Spaniards to pronounce, they called him El Greco, which means "the Greek." Before settling in the town of Toledo, he studied painting in Venice and learned how Venetian artists used color.

What a contrast there is between El Greco and Giorgione! El Greco did not soften his color changes as the Italian painter did. Nor did he use as much white to separate his vivid colors. Red is next to blue and next to orange. The two reds are different, and the orange tends to be more yellow than red. El Greco used a group of three colors—red, blue, and yellow—that has been repeated with variations over and over by artists through the centuries.

For each of his colors the artist used a light shade and a dark shade to suggest the folds of cloth. The folds reflect the streaks of bright light that seem to flicker from the stormy sky over the figures.

El Greco was not concerned with making the figures or colors look natural. He was an intense man who wanted to present the Bible stories in a stirring way, almost as though we were seeing visions of them. Visions, like dreams, never appear exactly real. Many things are exaggerated and changed. El Greco created an unreal world in his paintings, for he wanted to stir our feelings. His use of color greatly helped him to achieve success. We look at his pictures and experience sadness, joy, tenderness, and awe.

Holy Family   EL GRECO

The Cleveland Museum of Art, Cleveland, Ohio
GIFT OF FRIENDS OF THE MUSEUM

❧ COLOR

ORIENTAL ARTISTS emphasize color as pattern. They place colors in different parts of the picture to create a pleasing arrangement. On the opposite page is a reproduction of a Japanese print that was made in several steps. First, the artist painted the lines on paper. Then the block-cutter pasted the paper to a flat piece of wood and cut away the white parts, leaving the lines. The artist selected the colors to be used. The printer made the picture from the master block, and used a separate block for every color. He made many copies of each of the prints. They were so popular that some Japanese painters devoted their lives to designing pictures for reproduction in this manner.

This print shows two girls warming their feet as they play "cat's cradle." Notice the colors. A broad band of pink edges the brown blanket between them and joins the two girls together. (The blanket holds in the heat from a little stove under it.) One girl's kimono is pale blue with a large white design. The other girl wears a pink kimono with a very small design, but her blue and white sash in bold squares balances the other costume. There are two touches of yellow, one in the flower arrangement and one as a border for the painted screen.

Color as pattern is an important feature of this picture, which is delicate and at the same time elegant. Several Western artists, notably Vincent van Gogh and the American James McNeill Whistler, admired the use of color in Japanese prints.

Playing Cat's Cradle   SUZUKI HARUNOBU

Courtesy of the Metropolitan Museum of Art, New York

BEQUEST OF MRS. H. O. HAVEMEYER, 1929

THE H. O. HAVEMEYER COLLECTION

～ PATTERN

JAMES McNEILL WHISTLER's portrait of his mother introduces us to one of the five principles that control the five elements of painting. Whistler used the principle of *pattern* that has been mentioned in relation to color in Japanese art. Pattern is a controlling principle even in a work of art without color. Whistler called the picture on the opposite page ''Arrangement in Gray and Black.'' Actually he used several colors in subdued tones. The figure of his mother is part of the pattern of shapes that include the curtain, a picture on the wall, and the edge of another frame.

We realize how much Whistler admired oriental art when we see the way he placed the flat shapes in a very flat space. The mother, wearing a plain, full dress, is seated in profile. The wall behind her is pale, the baseboard is dark, and the floor is a medium tone. Her cap, handkerchief, and lace cuffs, together with the white mat of the picture and the sparkling design in the curtain, create a pattern of light against dark.

Whistler worked out this painting in a short stroke method similar to that Monet used, but Whistler blended his paint strokes. His painting is an impression rather than a sharp, realistic portrait. It is a quiet picture in soft, dark colors carefully observed under subdued light. He searched for ways to paint pictures with as little light as possible. He was particularly fond of misty days.

Whistler reduced the elements he used to *shape* and *light,* with few *lines,* little *space,* and neutral *color*. The pattern of light and dark shapes therefore became very important. He attained the great simplicity, restfulness, and dignity that we see in his portrait of his mother.

Mother of the Artist (Arrangement in Gray and Black)

JAMES McNEILL WHISTLER

Louvre, Paris, France

HENRI-JULIEN ROUSSEAU lived in Paris most of his life, and taught himself how to paint. When he was a young man in the French army, he visited the jungles of Central America. He never forgot this experience. Perhaps because he had no teacher for painting, his pictures are different from others we have seen. Moreover, he worked partly from memory of the things he had observed as a young man.

There is a fine zoo in Paris and there are botanical gardens also. Rousseau spent many days at both places, sketching animals and birds and studying plants. His sketches provided him with shapes and colors for the large jungle scenes he painted, such as *The Waterfall*. A screen of dense foliage almost hides the native figures and animals that are peering through the leaves. If you have ever been in a jungle, you will remember that you felt uneasy because the ferns and vines in your path were so huge they barred the way. You could not clearly see what was ahead. Great leaves blocked your view. You were sure that animals and savages lurked nearby without your knowing exactly where they were.

Rousseau wanted to impress us with the strangeness of the place and the feeling that it could almost swallow up people and animals. He could have painted a confused mass of leaves and branches. But, like all artists, he made a selection of only a few things to suggest the idea of the jungle. The plants in this picture are very large and look almost like trees. Each leaf is bold and clear, forming part of an over-all flat pattern that is a decoration for the surface of the canvas. Rousseau created the pattern by using the elements of *line, shape,* and *color.*

The Waterfall
Courtesy of the Art Institute of Chicago, Chicago, Illinois
HELEN BIRCH BARTLETT MEMORIAL COLLECTION

HENRI-JULIEN ROUSSEAU

Balance is an important principle of painting. Everything in a picture should balance: the lines and shapes, the dark and light pattern, the color pattern. If a picture has been painted off balance, we feel we would like to set it straight.

There is a kind of mechanical balancing like that of a seesaw when two persons of equal weight are seated, one on each end. The board is level; the people are balanced. MEINDERT HOBBEMA, a Dutch landscape artist, painted equal weights on either side of the road in this view of an avenue of trees. One side is almost like the other except for a few changes in shapes of buildings and their distance from us. Such balance gives a feeling of steadiness and calm. In this picture it permits the artist to concentrate our attention on the lines of the road and the treetops, growing ever nearer until they meet where the land joins the sky at the horizon. Pictures drawn in this way, with lines which grow nearer in the distance, are said to be drawn in linear perspective.

There is another form of perspective used by oriental artists. They employ oblique or slanting lines, as you can see in the Japanese print on page 43. When we first look at oriental pictures they seem peculiar, as if the upper part of the picture were tipped toward us. Once we become accustomed to looking at them, they seem balanced and pleasing.

Perspective is really an invention based on mathematics. It is used to create a feeling of space and distance.

The Avenue, Middleharnis
Reproduced by Courtesy of the Trustees
The National Gallery, London, England

MEINDERT HOBBEMA

[49]

HERE is a landscape that is a fine example of a kind of balance different from that used by Hobbema in his picture. JOHN CONSTABLE was an English artist admired for his carefully observed scenes of nature. This view of Salisbury Cathedral is one of many that he painted during visits over a period of eighteen years. He worked outdoors in all kinds of weather, and drew or painted the great church from every angle.

Like Monet, who admired the English artist's work and who also recorded a cathedral in numerous pictures, Constable was interested in the effects of light and air, the changing appearance of the church at different times of day in different lights.

The spire rises to the right of center. Trees frame it on either side. Notice that the tower is not exactly in the middle of the space between the trees. Some cows drink from the stream in the foreground. A path leads into space on the left. With his walking stick a gentleman points out some feature of the architecture to his companion.

Place one of your fingers over the lady and gentleman. You will see that the tower seems to move slightly to the right. This seeming shift is caused by Constable's use of the figures of the two people to balance the right-hand side of the picture. It is a curious fact that people in a painting, even though they are small, seemingly balance much larger objects. The feeling of balance comes about because we are all interested in seeing human beings in a picture. Our eyes seek them out and tend to linger on them.

Most artists use a form of balance similar to Constable's, placing a large shape on one side and smaller shapes on the other side in order to suggest life and movement, a feeling of active forces holding each other in balance.

Salisbury Cathedral from the Bishop's Garden   JOHN CONSTABLE
Copyright, The Frick Collection, New York

✎ BALANCE

A GREAT CHANGE took place in the art of painting when the camera was invented. Artists realized that photographs could show the appearance of the world. Little by little they began looking at things around them in a different way and creating new images.

PABLO PICASSO, a noted modern artist, is a Spaniard who has lived in France for many years. He was one of the first to take up new ideas about painting. In this picture we see three men wearing costumes and masks as if they were dressed for a Halloween party. There are two clowns and a monk with a rope around his waist. Each has a musical instrument and each has a mustache. The artist has broken up the various parts of the figures and their clothes and instruments into a pattern of shapes. The musicians' masks are askew. Their bodies seem to be made of squares. The white clown is the center of the painting. The two figures on either side balance each other. The monk is balanced by the triangular pattern in the suit of the clown on the left, the dark section in the middle of that costume, and the table top jutting out toward us.

The artist has also used other elements of painting. *Light* falls on the table and on the notes of music. The *space* is very shallow, but we can look beyond the figures to the wall decorated with a *pattern* of small crossed lines.

When you first looked at the picture, you may have thought it was jumbled. Perhaps now you will agree that it is organized, as other fine pictures are. Picasso obviously enjoyed painting it, and has given us a clear impression of three cheerful people having a good time making noisy music.

Three Musicians   PABLO PICASSO

Philadelphia Museum of Art, Philadelphia, Pennsylvania

A. E. GALLATIN COLLECTION

Rhythm, another principle of painting, suggests movement and life, the feeling of energy and force. Rhythm gives a picture motion. On the other hand, it does not destroy the impression of orderliness and careful arrangement that every fine picture must have.

It is easy to follow rhythm in music and it is easy to follow the rhythm of *The Wedding Dance,* painted by PIETER BRUEGHEL THE ELDER. We can almost hear the stamping of feet and the shouts as the partners swing one another in the country dance of old Belgium. It is a boisterous occasion, and the artist painted these peasant people in solid shapes. He repeated lines many times to carry our eyes around and about, in and out, from group to group. The dancing couples are blended together by interlocking curves.

The painting includes small details to emphasize the theme. The women's heavy skirts swirl in large folds; their aprons and white caps are edged and folded with fine, fluttering lines that suggest motion from the wind and the movements of the dance. Almost every inch of the picture is occupied, yet because of the careful arrangement it is not cluttered. The gestures of heads and arms and hands are repeated over and over again so that the gay rhythm is carried into the distance where a grove of trees offers rest for the dancers. Perhaps you can count the number of people in this painting and make a list of the different things that are going on.

Many of Brueghel's paintings show people having a good time, and express his joy in life and his fondness for his fellow men.

The Wedding Dance   PIETER BRUEGHEL THE ELDER
Courtesy of the Detroit Institute of Arts, Detroit, Michigan

JEAN ANTOINE WATTEAU was one of the great artists of France. He painted only a few pictures because he was ill most of his short life. *The Dance in a Pavilion* is full of a rhythm much gentler than the rhythm of Brueghel's *Wedding Dance*. Only one couple is dancing. Over them a high arch rises out of the picture so that we can see the beautiful landscape beyond.

The musicians form a trio at the left. Ladies and gentlemen form another group at the right. All of the figures are slim and elegant, and wear costly, rustling silks. A fountain sends up jets of water from a huge basin in the garden. We can imagine the warm breeze coming into the cool garden house, the air filled with perfumes and the sweet, soft sounds of music and conversation.

The two dancers sway and turn. Notice the curve of their upheld arms and the curve of the girl's figure as she leans away from her partner. His figure inclines toward her as he passes under their clasped hands. All of the costumes are ridged in little folds placed one next to the other with winding lines repeating the same small shapes. The lines suggest the movement of the people as well as the shimmer of light on their clothing. The light seems to come from the front as if from the footlights of a stage.

We think of Watteau as a court painter because he pictured ladies and gentlemen who lived in palaces with kings and queens. They could afford the sweet pleasure of doing nothing, and they did it with the refined grace that the artist expresses so well through his rhythmic lines.

The Dance in a Pavilion

JEAN ANTOINE WATTEAU

The Cleveland Museum of Art, Cleveland, Ohio

LOUIS D. BEAUMONT COLLECTION

ALBERT PINKHAM RYDER, an American artist, lived in New York City. He preferred the night to daytime. Occasionally he went out in a friend's boat and there, on the water under a full moon, he was inspired to return to his room and paint an impression of the night.

In *Toilers of the Sea* he has repeated many times the shallow curve of the ship's sail. Even the mast is slightly curved. The waves and clouds repeat the line over and over again and suggest the rhythm of the sound of waves and the rising and falling of the boat in regular motion on the sea.

You will recall *Fog Warning,* by Winslow Homer. In that painting we can see the man in the boat very clearly; he is close to us. Ryder places his boat and men much farther away so that the men are small shapes against the sky. Homer emphasized the strength of the man. Ryder emphasizes the strength of the boat. It sails along before the wind strongly and bravely, bearing its trusting human beings. Unlike Homer, who combined the grandeur of the sea with its danger, Ryder combined grandeur with a kind of steadfastness, like that of the moon, round and full, lighting the ship's path. Homer reported to us an exciting and possibly terrifying event: the fisherman threatened by the fog. Ryder painted a poem about the sea. He also wrote a poem to go with this picture.

> *With the shifting skies,*
> *Over the billowing foam,*
> *The hardy fisher flies*
> *To his island home.*

Toilers of the Sea   ALBERT PINKHAM RYDER
Addison Gallery of American Art, Phillips Academy, Andover, Massachusetts

✺ CONTRAST

Contrast is a principle controlling the elements of painting. All the elements must work together in harmonious relationship, but on the other hand, if the picture is too harmonious it appears weak or monotonous. Therefore the artist must create differences to give contrast. He must avoid too much contrast, though, in order not to destroy the harmony.

In this view of a Paris park on a sunny afternoon, by GEORGES SEURAT, most of the people face the water. They watch other people boating and fishing. Some, like the man in the foreground, are resting and daydreaming. There is repetition to create harmony. The curves and scallops of the parasols are repeated throughout, even by the dog's tail. The ladies' hats are almost all the same shape and so are the ladies themselves, with slim waists, full skirts, and tight jackets.

Seurat has also achieved harmony by placing his figures in a way to suggest order and calm. Each figure has its own space to itself except for the few in couples, who provide contrast. The artist created further contrast by his pattern of light and shade. The dark leaves of the trees form a band across the top. The people cast shadows pointing inward across the sunlit space.

Notice also the contrast of vertical and horizontal shapes. For the most part the figures are either standing or sitting upright rather stiffly. Their dark shapes, together with those of the trees, are at right angles to the shadow bands and the long, horizontal white line of the distant wall.

In this beautiful example of contrast Seurat created a painting that appears as flat as a fine wall decoration, yet at the same time suggests endless space.

Sunday Afternoon on the Island of La Grande Jatte   GEORGES SEURAT
The Art Institute of Chicago, Chicago, Illinois
THE HELEN BIRCH BARTLETT MEMORIAL COLLECTION

Las Meniñas by DIEGO VELÁZQUEZ is one of the world's famous paintings. It pictures the little Princess Margarita, two maids of honor, dwarfs, teachers, and the grand marshal of the Spanish court standing in the doorway. The artist himself is also in the painting, pausing for a moment from work on a large canvas. On the back wall, dimly seen in a mirror, are the faces of the king and queen. There are nine persons and a dog in the picture, yet it does not seem crowded.

Velázquez was an expert at picturing both filled and empty space. Here the people are grouped in the foreground, except for the grand marshal who is placed far back in the picture. We feel that there is a great distance between him and the others.

The light is also indicated with great skill. It filters in from high, partly shuttered windows and reveals the artist, the princess, her maids, and the dwarfs. The middle of the room is darker. At the back, bright light streams in through the open door.

This picture is a fine example of the principle of *unity*: the proper relation of all parts to the whole. Further, Velázquez followed the principle of *contrast*. He wished to emphasize the little princess and the group around her by balancing their shapes with mysterious, shadowy space. The artist expressed his view of the scene with this combination of a clear foreground and an indistinct background. The room did not actually look this way, but he gives us his impression of the scene according to his feeling for light and space.

Las Meniñas (Maids of Honor)   DIEGO VELÁZQUEZ
Prado, Madrid, Spain

BEFORE the camera was invented, people were portrayed by artists who specialized in such pictures, called portraits. Even today a few persons have their portraits painted, but usually they ask a photographer to record their appearance.

Sir ANTHONY VAN DYCK was one of the finest of portrait artists. He was knighted in recognition of his splendid pictures of kings and queens and other nobility. Although he was born and studied in Belgium, he traveled a great deal and went as far as Genoa, Italy, to paint the Marchesa Grimaldi. The Marchesa gives us a passing glance as she leaves her palace to go down the garden steps. A young Moorish attendant holds a parasol over her head to protect her fair face from the burning sun. The artist painted the lady life-size. He may even have increased her height to emphasize her dignity. She is dressed in a rich black gown trimmed with gold. Her parasol is scarlet, and the palace is built of golden-colored stone.

This painting is a fine example of unity. The *lines, shapes, space, light,* and *colors* are balanced with each other to give a splendid effect. Much of the effect comes from the way the artist applied paint to canvas. He overlaid transparent colors which we look through to the colors underneath. The tints of the lady's skin glow with the same colors as they did when she was alive. The sky is like a rich tapestry of cloud and light, an effect achieved with delicate tints.

The luxurious use of oil paint in this portrait is most appropriate and helps to create a unified work of art.

Marchesa Elena Grimaldi, Wife of Marchese Nicola Cattaneo
Sir ANTHONY VAN DYCK

National Gallery of Art, Washington, D. C.
WIDENER COLLECTION

The Madonna of the Chair is a fine example of unity. The picture is unusual in many respects, but particularly because the figures are painted on a circular canvas. The heads are almost like portraits and we feel that the artist, RAPHAEL, must have asked an Italian mother to bring her baby to his studio to pose while he sketched and painted.

It was necessary for the artist to make several practice drawings in order to arrange the three figures perfectly within the circle. In one of the sketches the baby is sitting up straight. In another the mother is leaning back. Neither of these positions would have suited the circle, so Raphael tried various others until the figures related well to each other and to the whole picture. The artist finally arrived at a perfect balance around the center. There are many curves, worked out in a variety of ways: the curving line of the mother's arm, the pattern of her dress, the folds of material around her head, the position of the young Saint John looking toward the Christ Child, all done so that our eyes will not stray outside the circle.

Raphael realized that his shapes, no matter how carefully he arranged them, might appear to be rolling in a wheel, so he used the straight shape of the chair post to hold his picture steady.

There is another unusual feature of the painting: the mother is looking out of the canvas toward us. Her fondness for her child is surely felt in the way her head is close to his. The soft, even light, the compact space, and the rich, warm colors of the original painting all show us how well Raphael could picture ideal perfection.

The Madonna of the Chair
Gallery of the Pitti Palace, Florence, Italy

RAPHAEL

YOU HAVE READ that Picasso was one of the first modern artists to take up new ideas about painting. Here we have a work by the Dutch painter, PIET MONDRIAN, who experimented along different lines and arrived at different results. Because he believed that a painting did not require a subject, his paintings do not remind us of anything we have seen before. This example of his work is called *Composition in White, Red, and Black*. It is made up of the same elements and follows the same principles that the other pictures in this book do. The result is a fine example of *unity*. *Line* of slightly different thicknesses creates *shape*. *Space* is in two equal dimensions because the picture is square. Since there is no frame to enclose the painting, we can imagine that the lines and the white square extend out into space, off the edges of the page.

At moments, as we look steadily, certain of the rectangles seem to advance or retreat slightly, so that there is a suggestion of the third dimension of depth. There is *balance, contrast,* and even *rhythm* in the lines placed close together, as they repeat themselves and the enclosed shapes with ever so slight differences.

Mondrian followed a path blazed by Cézanne and Picasso. The path brought him to what we call "abstract painting." He completely freed himself of having to select something to start with. He did not have to worry about the confusion and disorder of things in the world about him. He expressed order—the order in the mind of man that creates music, mathematics, and architecture.

Take a square of paper and some black strips and try to arrange them as precisely as Mondrian did. You will be surprised to discover how delicately balanced his painting is.

Composition in White, Black, and Red   Piet Mondrian

The Museum of Modern Art, New York

GIFT OF THE ADVISORY COMMITTEE